Helen Exley Giftbooks
for the most thoughtful gifts of all

OTHER BOOKS IN THIS SERIES:

For a wonderful Mother A book to make your own

For a wonderful Grandmother A book to make your own

For a real Friend A book to make your own

A Woman's Journal A personal notebook and keepsake

Cats A book to make your own

Teddy Bears A book to make your own

Inspirations A book to make your own

A Gardener's Journal A book to make your own

OTHER HELEN EXLEY GIFTBOOKS
FOR GIRLS:

Girls Address Book

To a very special Friend

My Daughter, my joy...

Sisters! A Little Giftbook

Congratulations on your Graduation

Published in hardback 1990. Published in softcover 2001.
Copyright © Helen Exley 1990, 2001
Selection © Helen Exley 1990, 2001
The moral right of the author has been asserted.

12 11 10 9 8 7 6 5 4 3 2

ISBN 1-86187-215-1

Selection and design by Helen Exley
Illustrated by Juliette Clarke
Printed in China

Exley Publications Ltd, 16 Chalk Hill, Watford, Herts, WD1 4BN, UK.
Exley Publications LLC, 232 Madison Avenue, Suite 1409, NY 10016, USA.

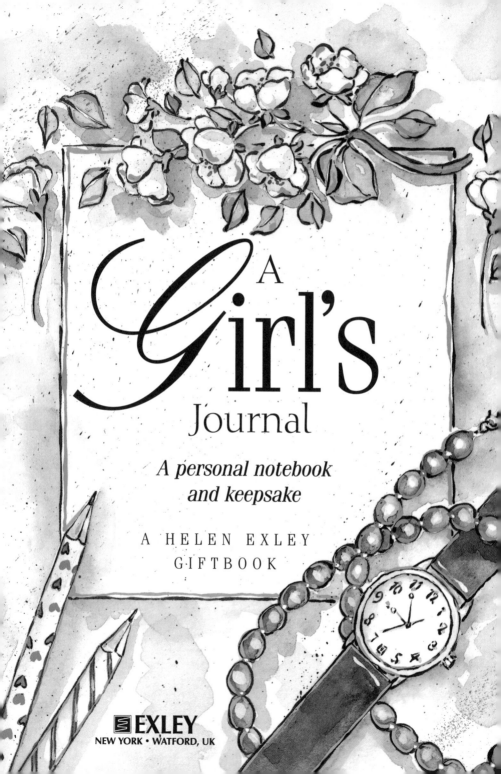

A Girl's Journal

Journal

A personal notebook and keepsake

A HELEN EXLEY
GIFTBOOK

EXLEY
NEW YORK • WATFORD, UK

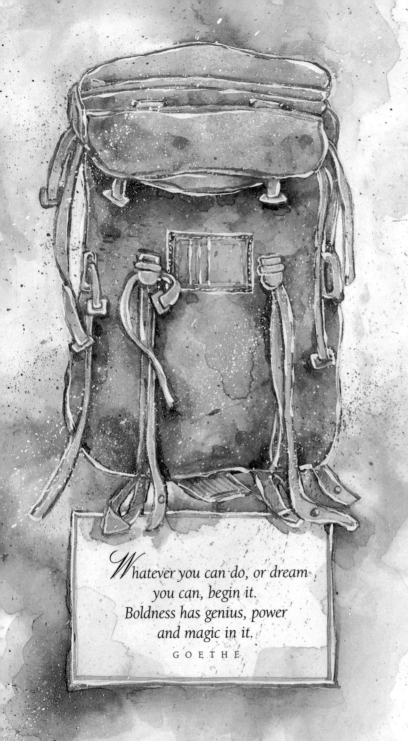

Whatever you can do, or dream
you can, begin it.
Boldness has genius, power
and magic in it.

GOETHE

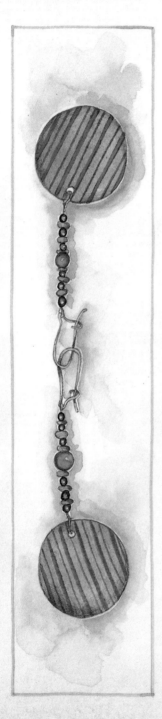

$\mathcal{T}$here are two sorts of girl.
The one who feels embarrassed
that all eyes are on her.
And the one who is happily
convinced that they are.

SAMANTHA ARMSTRONG

Stand firm in your refusal
to remain conscious during Algebra.
In real life, I assure you,
there is no such thing as Algebra.

FRAN LEBOWITZ

Everyone has their special gift.
In some it is speech, in some, silence.
The world has need of small perfections
as well as great achievements.

PAM BROWN

The world is made of people
who never quite get into the first team
and who just miss the prizes
at the flower show.

J. BRONOWSKI FROM,
"THE ASCENT OF MAN"

*L*ove is lunacy. What else would make me keep an empty tin of cola, a used Bandaid, a bus ticket and a bitten pencil stub.

CHARLOTTE GRAY

Forget-me-nots

for ~
· remembrance ·

❧ Sage ❧

~ symbolizes
mutual love ·

❧ Thyme ❧

~ symbolizes
Sweetness ~

Periwinkle

· for · ~ ·
happy memories

There are muddled kisses
and clever kisses.
The muddled ones
are usually the ones
you remember forever.

SAMANTHA ARMSTRONG

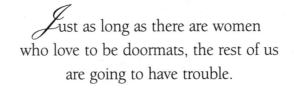

*J*ust as long as there are women
who love to be doormats, the rest of us
are going to have trouble.

ANONYMOUS

I can hand on very little wise advice.
But remember from the start of any relationship
every man is potentially capable of
making a pot of tea and cooking an
acceptable meal. And nothing in the male
make-up prevents them sewing on buttons.

M.C.G.

The way you overcome shyness
is to become so wrapped up in something
that you forget to be afraid.

LADY BIRD JOHNSON

It's wonderful to be looked after
— but it's even more wonderful
to be able to look after yourself.

JESSE O'NEILL

N O WOMAN CAN CALL HERSELF FREE WHO
DOES NOT OWN AND CONTROL HER OWN BODY.

MARGARET SANGER

In a world that seems dominated by greed
and selfishness and cruelty, there are always
enough people sitting on pavements,
carrying banners, picketing embassies, signing
petitions, making speeches, cornering politicians
and setting up organizations to give the heart
a little hope.

PAM BROWN

DAUGHTERS ARE NOT THE CHANCE
TO DO A CORRECTIVE RE-RUN
ON ONE'S OWN MISGUIDED YOUTH.
THEY WANT THEIR OWN MISGUIDED YOUTH.

PAM BROWN

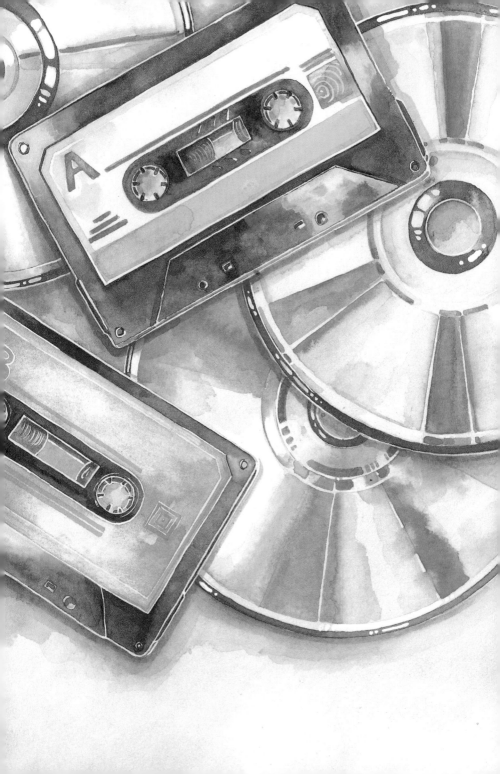

Just when the world seems chained forever
in dark and cold, up bobs the next generation,
brash and bright as daffodils.

HELEN THOMSON

*M*istakes are necessary.
Embarrassment is necessary.
How else can we learn?
How else can we discover
the necessities of patience,
kindness, sympathy and
forgiveness?

CLARA ORTEGA

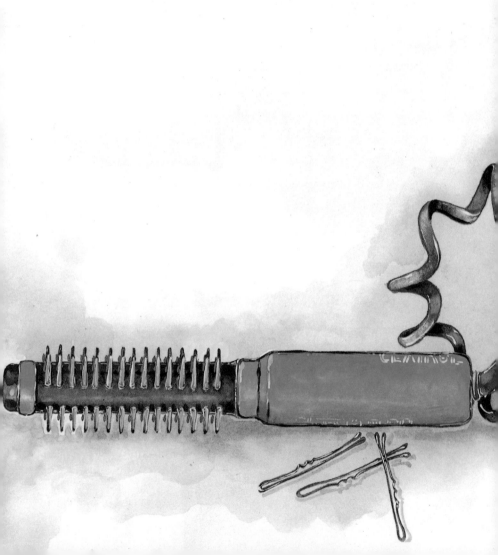

Why not be oneself?
That is the whole secret of a successful appearance.
If one is a greyhound, why try to look
like a Pekinese?

EDITH SITWELL

No one is "free".
That would be to live in total isolation.
We are woven into every other life
and must recognize this fact if the planet
is to survive.

PETER GRAY

An adult woman
is one who does not think
predominantly of
her sex, but of her humanity.

W.C. FAITH

*Examinations are passed on coffee, toffees, peanuts
and jam butties. It is hard to possess
both a finely honed mind and a finely honed body.*

PATRICIA HITCHCOCK

He loves
·me·
He loves
·me not·

Why does the most vital learning period
of one's life coincide with
a blinding obsession with the opposite sex?

M.C.G.

SUCCESS IS NOT FAME OR MONEY.
IT IS TO HAVE CREATED SOMETHING
VALUABLE FROM YOUR OWN
INDIVIDUALITY AND SKILL —
A GARDEN, AN EMBROIDERY, A PAINTING.
A LIFE.

CHARLOTTE GRAY

Some boys say it with chocolate.
But the best present is some oddity you mentioned in passing,
that he's spent three lunch times searching for.

SUSAN MILLARD

*If you can react the same way to winning and losing,
that's a big accomplishment.*

CHRIS EVERT

*Risk! Risk anything! Care no more for the opinions
of others, for those voices. Do the hardest thing on earth
for you. Act for yourself. Face the truth.*

KATHERINE MANSFIELD

As long as femininity is associated with ruffles
and flourishes and a lack of directness
and honesty... (women) are never praised without
being patronised. Their jacket photographs
are reviewed instead of their books.

ERICA JONG

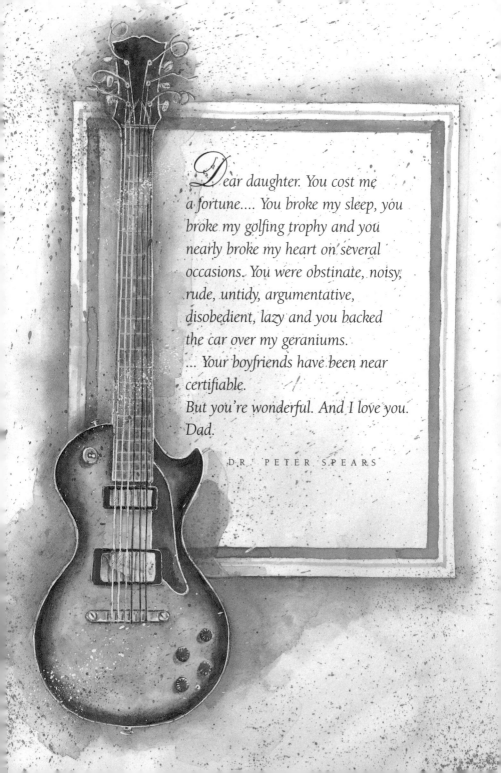

Dear daughter. You cost me a fortune.... You broke my sleep, you broke my golfing trophy and you nearly broke my heart on several occasions. You were obstinate, noisy, rude, untidy, argumentative, disobedient, lazy and you backed the car over my geraniums.

... Your boyfriends have been near certifiable.

But you're wonderful. And I love you. Dad.

DR. PETER SPEARS

$\mathcal{B}$ecome a true expert in something.
Anything. Then the question of you being a woman
will barely raise its head.

DR. JANINE COOPER

Macho male dancers, gentle male nurses, dominant
female Prime Ministers, gutsy female archaeologists.
At last a world where it's ability that counts, not sex.
We're not there yet but watch this space....

PAM BROWN

No ONE CAN MAKE YOU FEEL INFERIOR
WITHOUT YOUR OWN CONSENT.

ELEANOR ROOSEVELT

THERE IS NO SUCH THING AS "GIRL", "WOMAN", "BOY", "MAN".
THERE ARE MILLIONS OF TOTALLY INDIVIDUAL HUMAN BEINGS.
START YOUR CAMPAIGN FROM THERE.

ROSANNE AMBROSE-BROWN

*Coffee in the kitchen, shoeless and exhausted
after a hard day's shopping,
patches up a multitude of differences between
a daughter and her mum.*

PAM BROWN

Never grow a wishbone, daughter, where your backbone ought to be.

CLEMENTINE PADDLEFORD

IF AT FIRST YOU DON'T SUCCEED,
TRY AGAIN. THEN QUIT.
NO USE BEING A DAMN FOOL ABOUT IT.

W. C. FIELDS

*O*nly good girls keep diaries.
Bad girls don't have the time.

TALLULAH BANKHEAD

You can take no credit for beauty at sixteen. But if you are beautiful at 60, it will be your own soul's doing.

MARIE STOPES

Taking joy in life is a woman's best cosmetic.

ROSALIND RUSSELL

*Love is walking two miles
out of your way
just to pass his gate.
Even if you know he's not there.*

SAMANTHA ARMSTRONG

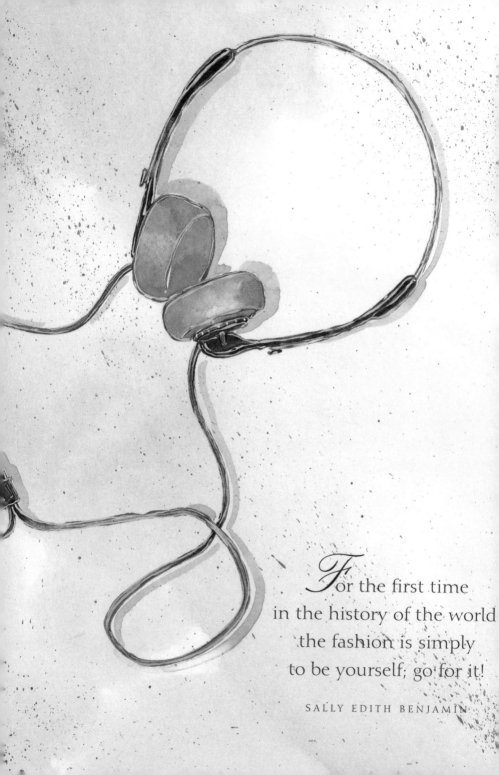

For the first time
in the history of the world
the fashion is simply
to be yourself; go for it!

SALLY EDITH BENJAMIN

Young people do not know enough to be prudent, and therefore they attempt the impossible – and achieve it, generation after generation.

PEARL BUCK

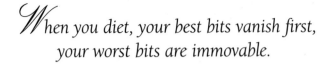

*When you diet, your best bits vanish first,
your worst bits are immovable.*

CHARLOTTE GRAY

*It's no good tiptoeing
up to the bathroom scales dear.
They hear you coming.*

PAM BROWN

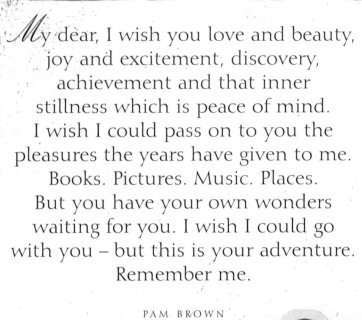

My dear, I wish you love and beauty,
joy and excitement, discovery,
achievement and that inner
stillness which is peace of mind.
I wish I could pass on to you the
pleasures the years have given to me.
Books. Pictures. Music. Places.
But you have your own wonders
waiting for you. I wish I could go
with you – but this is your adventure.
Remember me.

PAM BROWN

HOW MANY YOUNG
PEOPLE EMBARK UPON LIFE WITH A TEDDY
IN THEIR CASE!
PAM BROWN

*The purpose of life,
after all, is to live it, to taste
experience to the utmost,
to reach out eagerly
and without fear for newer
and richer experience.*

ELEANOR ROOSEVELT

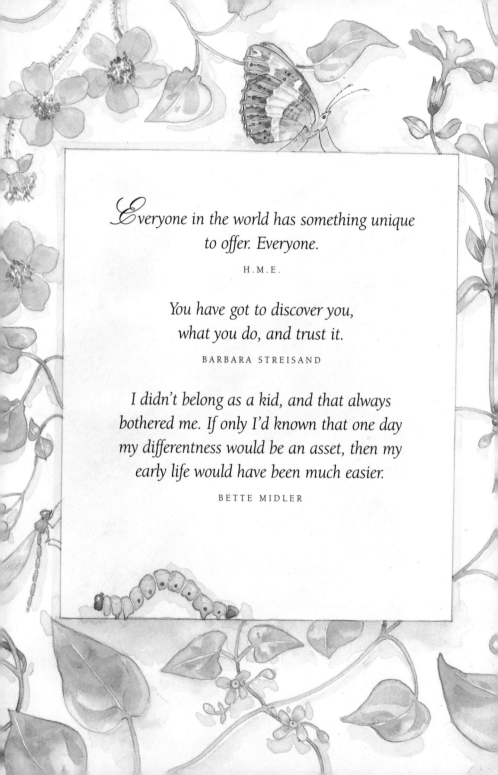

Everyone in the world has something unique to offer. Everyone.

H.M.E.

*You have got to discover you,
what you do, and trust it.*

BARBARA STREISAND

*I didn't belong as a kid, and that always
bothered me. If only I'd known that one day
my differentness would be an asset, then my
early life would have been much easier.*

BETTE MIDLER

You will do foolish things
but do them with enthusiasm.

COLETTE